LILLENAS®

Easter

PROGRAM BUILDER

NO. 36

Creative Resources for Program Directors

Compiled by HEIDI PETAK

lillenas
PUBLISHING COMPANY
Kansas City, MO 64141

Questions? Please write or call:
Lillenas Publishing Company
Drama Resources
P. O. Box 419527
Kansas City, MO 64141
Phone: 816-931-1900 • Fax: 816-412-8390
E-mail: drama@lillenas.com
Web Site: www.lillenasdrama.com

Executive Editor: Heidi Petak
Copy Editor: Kimberly Meiste
Manuscript Formatting: Karen Phillips
Cover Design by Sharon Page

Contents

Recitations for Children

Surprise!

We love surprises
When Mommy sneaks up to tickle me,
Surprise!
When Daddy hides and then jumps out,
Surprise!
But the best surprise was when every-
thing was very quiet;
Shhh. *(Children put their index fingers
to their lips and crouch down)*
For one day, *(put up one finger)*
Two days, *(put up two fingers)*
Three days, *(put up three fingers)*
And then, *(children rise up suddenly
with their arms in the air)*
Surprise!
Jesus is alive!

by Lauren West

Thank You, God

Thank You, God, for making trees.
Thank You, God, for making me.
Thank You, God, for raining showers.
Thank You, God, for growing flowers.
Thank You, God, for painting colors.
Thank You, God, for creating mothers.
Thank You, God, for giving breath.
Thank You, God, for reversing death.
Thank You, God, for life today.
Thank You, God, we all can say,
Happy Easter!

by April Kelly

The New Coat

Whenever I got new clothes, I got them
from my brothers—
Seven older boys who pass their clothes
to one another.

Since I'm the youngest one, all my
clothes are old and worn,
And sometimes they don't smell good,
and some are ripped or torn!

But one day, Mother worked—she
stitched and cut and sewed,
And finally, I had a coat that wasn't
used and old!

I put my coat on happily and walked
right into town.
I wanted everyone to see me as I
proudly walked around.

But nobody would look at me. They all
ran out the gate.
"It's Jesus," they were calling. "Hurry,
don't be late!"

So I ran, too, to see Him—the One who
healed the lame.
I heard He was the Son of God and
down the road He came!

"Let's make a special carpet!" the people
near me cried.
And then they took their coats off and
laid them side-by-side.

My new coat, my brand new coat! Oh,
what was I to do?
I laid it down for Jesus. You would have
done that too.

by Beth Swale

Easter Egg Hunt

I'm hunting with my basket,
I'm running with my legs.
I'm looking for some treasure,
Those little Easter eggs.

And just like seeking treasure
I'm seeking all that's true.
I know Jesus is alive,
And He rose for me and you!

by Lauren West

Christ Is Risen!

Awake! Awake!
And don't be sad,
Today is *Easter Day!*
Christ is risen!
Alive and well!
So join with us and say,
He's Alive!
(All together) He's Alive!

by Dorothy Heibel

Disciples All Waiting

(Children clap as they say each number)
Disciples all waiting—one, two, three.
Hiding in the dark, scared as can be.
Jesus on the cross—four and five,
Was He still dead? Was He alive?
Everyone quiet—six, seven, eight.
What if guards come and knock at the
      gate?
Mary comes running—nine and ten,
She says, "Jesus is *alive* again!"

Peter and John run—one, two, three,
If He's alive they want to see!
Looking in the tomb—four and five,
Jesus is gone—is He alive?
Disciples all wondering—six, seven,
      eight,
How long will they have to wait?
Jesus appears—nine and ten,
Jesus is with His friends again!
Disciples all rejoicing—one, two, three,
Jesus is alive for you and me!

by Beth Swale

What Did the Guards See?

What did the guards see on Easter morning?
Did they see a stone roll away without any warning?
Did they see an angel as bright as the sun?
Did they see all that and want to run?

What did the guards feel as Jesus rose?
Did they feel the earth shake beneath their toes?
Did they feel the stone roll like a giant wheel?
Did they freeze in shock wondering if it was all real?

What did the guards know on that day?
Did they know God's Son was the One in the grave?
Did they know they too were ones He came to save?
Did they hear their hearts pound as they fainted in fear?
Did they hear the angel shout, "*He is not here!*"

by Beth Swale

Jesus' Friends

Jesus' friends all cried
The day their Savior died.

All their hopes were lost
As He was taken off the cross.

They gathered in a room,
For three days watched His tomb.

The women went at dawn
To put their spices on.

But the stone was rolled away
That happy Easter day!

And Jesus' friends all cheered,
"He is risen! He is here!"

by April Kelly

Eastertide

A greening earth awakens
From its long winter sleep.
All signs of spring remind us
Of God's promises He keeps.
Arise, behold the beauty
Of God, our Savior's grace,
And praise Him for this Easter
That we'll one day see His face.

by Dorothy Heibel

I Believe

I believe that Jesus healed the sick and
raised the dead.
I believe that Jesus loved the world for
which He bled.
I believe that Jesus' frame lay in a tomb
three days.
I believe He rose again for me to give
Him praise!

by Noelle Nelson

The Gift of Life

(A reading for 5 STUDENTS)

STUDENT 1: I look around at our world
today and see chaos,

STUDENT 2: Sadness,

STUDENT 3: Anger,

STUDENT 4: Grief,

STUDENT 5: Hatred,

STUDENT 1: Judgment,

STUDENT 3: Fear,

STUDENT 5: Shame,

ALL: Death.

STUDENT 2: And I start thinking
all is lost,

STUDENT 4: Pointless,

STUDENT 1: Worthless,

ALL: Hopeless. *(Bow heads)*

STUDENT 3 *(lifts head):* But then
I remember,

STUDENT 5 *(lifts head):* That's why Jesus
died,

STUDENT 2 *(lifts head):* To free me
from shame,

STUDENT 4 *(lifts head):* To free me
from hatred,

STUDENT 1 *(lifts head):* To free me
from death.

STUDENT 3: And that's why He rose
again.

STUDENT 2: To give me joy.

STUDENT 5: To give me peace.

STUDENT 4: To give me hope.

ALL: To give us life.

STUDENT 3: Life.

STUDENT 5: Life.

STUDENT 1: Life.

ALL: Life!

by Noelle Nelson

Adult Readings

There's More to Easter
by Elaine Hardt

Easter bunnies and eggs a tradition,
A token visit to church mere cliché;
Families shopping in preparation
For just another busy holiday.

Remember Passover, the slaves set free,
The blood of a lamb placed on their door;
Obedience to God was freedom's key.
Let the Scriptures tell you more.

Messiah, Jesus, Lamb of God was slain,
Innocent, redeeming us from sin.
Death could not hold Him, He rose again.
To receive Him begins a new life within.

Some celebrate Easter in other ways.
Let your heart find the deeper reason.
For God's great love, let us give Him praise,
Embrace Him in this holy season.

A Gilded Thorn
by J. Bernadette Williamson

Oh thorn
    From my Redeemer's brow
You sting
    With love's tenacity,
Burning your stamp
    Of ownership
Upon these pulsing walls
    In me.
Golgotha's fury
    Buried deep

Within this frail
    And beating clay,
What privilege
    To share the scorn
That tore the hands
    So freely splayed.

The hero
    Holds his trophy high,
The crowd applauds
    And wildly chants.

I hold my trophy
In the depths
Where Christ
Is my sole audience.
More glorious
Than acclamation
From the worldly
Multitude
Is this seal
Of affirmation
Granted by
Great solitude.

Thus I wear
A badge of honor,

Hung upon
The deepest deep,
By the hands
Of my Beloved
Where only His gaze
Can reach.
Piercing pain
Of Passion's pleasure
Golden spike
Of irony,
Make us one
By Your desire,
Soften . . .
By sovereign agony.

The Power of Easter
by Heidi Petak

In the shadows the enemy lurks,
His appetite whet for destruction,
His eyes gleam,
Conniving lies,
Wrecking homes,
Killing love.
His crowning achievement:
God on a cross,
Broken,
Thundering,
Lightning flashing.

The power of the ages,
The power of love.

This power cannot be quenched,
It cannot be stopped;
It cannot be killed.

As God takes His sword from its sheath
The enemy cowers,
Watches,
Retreats.

And Creator steps into the tomb,
Breathes the breath of love
into broken flesh;
Sparks the lifeless heart of His Son
with a touch.

Beat, beat. Beat, beat.

Sends the blood coursing through veins,
Heals the pierced side
and nail-scarred hands.
Sight to eyes, sound to ears,
Shrugging off linens
Stained and needless.

Standing, walking,
bursting forth into morning light.
The tomb is empty,
The enemy defeated,
The Savior is risen!
Hallelujah!

Readers Theatre for Good Friday

All

by Allison Allen

Movement 1

ACTOR 1: Over five thousand times, one little word marks the pages of Scripture.

ACTOR 2: There is not one, single book in the whole of the Bible that does not contain it.

ACTOR 3: From Genesis to Revelation, there it is—one vowel and two twin consonants meaning:

ACTOR 4: enough, whole,

ACTOR 5: completely, entirely,

ACTOR 6: everything, everywhere.

ACTOR 7: A small word whose meaning is anything but small.

ACTOR 8: All.

ALL: All.

(Pause)

Movement 2

(Done as one overlapping sentence, very little pause between ACTORS.*)*

ACTOR 6: God saw all that He made, and it was good.

ACTOR 7: I am making between you and Me a covenant for all generations.

ACTOR 1: Noah did all that the Lord commanded him.

ACTOR 3: Come, all you who are thirsty.

ACTOR 8: For You created all things.

ACTOR 2: All the people will know,

ACTOR 5: I have gathered all the earth.

THE CHRIST: Behold I make all things new.

ACTOR 4: That you would prosper in all things.

ACTOR 6: All the people will know.

ACTOR 3: The same anointing teaches you all things.

ACTOR 4: He would that all should come to repentance.

ACTOR 7: Peace to you all,

ACTOR 1: Being strengthened with all power.

ACTOR 8: His divine power has given us all things.

ACTOR 2: All the prophets testify about Him.

ACTOR 5: Give ear, all you from far off countries,

ACTOR 4: All nations shall come and worship.

ACTOR 3: Being all things to all men.

ACTOR 6: All of you be of one mind.

ACTOR 2: Honor all people.

ACTOR 8: Cast all your care on Him for He cares for you.

ACTOR 5: They forsook all and followed Him.

ACTOR 3: In Him there is no darkness at all.

ACTOR 1: The grace of our Lord Jesus Christ be with you all.

(Pause)

THE CHRIST: God was pleased to have all His fullness dwell in Jesus, and through Jesus, to reconcile to Himself all things by making peace through Jesus' blood, shed on the cross.

Movement 3

(Transitional/expositional—there can be a bit more space in this section.)

ACTOR 1: The Father gave the Son all power, all fullness, all authority,

ACTOR 4: all wisdom, all grace, and all dominion.

ACTOR 3: And, two thousand years ago, on a dark, God-forsaken hill, when even the angels held their breath, the Father gave His beloved, begotten, only Son . . . all sin.

ACTOR 7: Jesus, the all in all.

ACTOR 2: Jesus, the One for all.

THE CHRIST: Father, if there is any other way, please let this cup pass from me.

ACTOR 1: All of us like sheep have gone astray,

ACTOR 5: and the Lord has laid on Him the iniquity of us all.

THE CHRIST: Father, if it is not possible for this cup to be taken away unless I drink it . . .

ACTOR 2: It was not possible.

ACTOR 5: It was the Father's will to crush Him,

ACTOR 7: To lay on Him the iniquity of us all.

THE CHRIST: Thy will be done.

(Beat)

Movement 4

(Once into the rhyme scheme, allow things to clip with clarity and rhythm. Go with the rhyme.)

ACTOR 5: The whole, completely, entirely, everything, everywhere . . .

ACTOR 3: Of sin.

ACTOR 6: All sin.

ACTOR 8: He, who knew no sin, became sin for

ALL: us.

ACTOR 1: Jesus, the Christ, became

ACTOR 6: genocide,

ACTOR 3: ghetto atrocities . . .

ACTOR 7: coarse jesting,

ACTOR 2: and false humility,

ACTOR 5: pride and petty jealously,

ACTOR 8: pill-popping and ruthless greed.

ACTOR 4: The man, the woman, the student who cheats,

THE CHRIST: All have sinned . . .

ACTOR 7: Cain's first strike,

ACTOR 1: Darfur's plight,

ACTOR 4: 1.5 billion unborn babies' lives . . .

THE CHRIST: And fallen short of the glory of God.

ACTOR 6: The earth soaked in innocents' stain,

ACTOR 3: 262 million silenced by Hitler, Stalin, Amine, Hussein,

THE CHRIST: If you hate your brother you are guilty of murder.

ACTOR 2: I have hated just the same.

ACTOR 5: Withheld love and silent praise,

ACTOR 4: Unforgiveness, unjust rage,

ACTOR 6: Gossip as prayer disguised,

ACTOR 1: A lying tongue, a haughty eye.

THE CHRIST: He who says he has no sin is a liar, and the truth is not in him.

ACTOR 7: The disease of sin's fall-out.

ACTOR 8: Double-minded, crushing doubt

ACTOR 3: For the user who forgets her own name

ACTOR 5: And the abuser who feels no shame.

THE CHRIST: Father, why have You forsaken Me?

ACTOR 1: For modern day rebels and church-bred Pharisees

ACTOR 3: Under steeples,

ACTOR 4: In chapels,

ACTOR 8: For warlords and kings.

ACTOR 2: In pulpits,

ACTOR 6: For pundits,

ACTOR 7: Prophets and politicians,

ACTOR 5: Little white lies and secret ambition.

HALF: Home-wreckers,

HALF: Home-makers,

ACTOR 3: For normal, good folk

ACTOR 1: And wounded God-haters.

(Beat)

ALL *(spoken in round)*: For you. For me. For we. For you. For me. For we. For us.

THE CHRIST: For God—the Father—so loved the world that He gave His only begotten Son, and laid on Him the sins of us all . . .

And Jesus took up His cross and carried it, for us . . .

ACTOR 6: All

ACTOR 1, 2, 3, 5 *(adding voices)*: All

ACTOR 4, 6, 7, 8 *(adding voices)*: All

ALL: All

Sketch for Children

Resurrection Reflections
by Linda J. Axom

Running Time: Approximately 3 to 5 minutes

Cast:
> LILLY
> STONE
> CLOTH

Props:
> Christ candle
> White cloth
> Gray cloth
> Off-white cloth

(An unlit Christ candle is set in place. A white cloth is worn over the head and/or shoulders of LILY; *a gray cloth is worn by* STONE; *and an off-white cloth is worn by* CLOTH. *The Christ candle is lit at the end of the piece. A bell choir or other musical instruments/choir may play an Easter piece at the end of the scene.)*

LILY: I am a beautiful, white lily. I have been growing beside a tomb. Wait! Someone is coming. Men. Carrying a body inside. And now . . . soldiers. Rolling a huge stone in front of the tomb. Now they are making sure the stone can't be moved. I wonder what they are so afraid of?

CLOTH: I am the cloth that is wrapped around the body of Jesus. For three days, I have been a covering for my Lord's body. He is cold, still, and lifeless. But . . . wait. Something is moving! It's Jesus! He is rising, gently taking off my bindings! Folding me and laying me neatly in a pile!

STONE: I am the stone sealing the tomb. I am heavy and unmovable. Or so I thought. My Lord is speaking. I am being rolled away! Jesus is leaving His grave!

LILY: The night is quiet, except for the usual night sounds. Crickets. Birds. Wind. My blossoms are drinking in the dew. The mist is thick and I am soaking it up! The sun is about to rise. Now it is daybreak. But what is that sound? I think it is a woman weeping.

CLOTH: I hear it too! She sounds pitifully brokenhearted! I think she is looking for Jesus!

STONE: A man is speaking to her. It is our Lord. But she doesn't recognize Him. She thinks He is the gardener and that He has taken Jesus away.

14

LILY: I know. But listen! He just called her by name, "Mary!" Her eyes were opened. Now she knows who He is!

CLOTH: She just called Him, "Master!" Where's she going now? I think she is running to tell the good news to Peter and the others!

STONE: Can you imagine that when the Lord calls us by name, our eyes will be opened and our lives will be changed forever?

LILY: I like imagining that! Look! Here comes Peter! Hey! He almost stepped on me! I think he ran here to see if it really was true that our Lord has risen and is now alive.

CLOTH: Peter came right into the tomb and now he sees me. He sees that I am all that is left inside. You should see the look on his face!

LILY: He is amazed and struck with awe!

STONE: Peter and the others were with Jesus throughout His ministry and had seen all His miracles; they had listened to His words. But even then they didn't understand all that He had said to them about His life and His destiny.

CLOTH: Even now they still don't understand it all, but they feel a glorious excitement and relief in just knowing that their Friend and their Lord lives again!

LILY: Now they wonder how much more is yet to unfold?

STONE: Jesus knew what His destiny was to be. Because of His unconditional love, He willingly went to the cross and was crucified for the sins of the entire world.

CLOTH: He conquered death and the grave and He lives now with His Father in heaven! All who believe in Him shall not perish but have everlasting life with Him.

LILY: God is so good! As the Lily, my blooms will hold their heads high to proclaim the mystery of God's plan of salvation to all people!

STONE: As the Stone, I will proclaim that the tomb is now empty!

CLOTH: As the Cloth, I will shout that my Savior lives again!

LILY: Let us spread the good news throughout the entire world!

STONE/CLOTH/LILY *(as they exit):* He is alive! He is alive! Jesus Christ lives today!

(Christ candle is lit. Choir or instruments play Easter piece such as "Christ the Lord Is Risen Today.")

Sketch for Teens

The Sketch

by Dave Tippett

Running Time: Approximately 4 to 5 minutes

Themes: Easter, Sin, Redemption

Scripture: Matthew 9:13

Synopsis: A playwright struggles with how to best dramatize the consequences of our actions and God's ultimate love.

Cast:
> PLAYWRIGHT—Woman or man, any age; dressed casually
> TEEN 1—Male; dressed in black
> TEEN 2—Female; dressed in black
> TEEN 3—Male; dressed in black

Props:
> Simple table
> Computer (laptop or desktop)
> Chair
> 1 red sock
> 1 white sock
> Black marker (non-permanent)
> Black fabric
> White fabric

Stage Direction Key:
> SL = stage left
> SR = stage right
> USC = upstage center
> CS = center stage
> DS = downstage
> DSL = downstage left
> DSR = downstage right

Production Notes: The teens are, in essence, acting out what the Playwright types. Playwright is never aware of their presence, although the teens are aware of Playwright's presence. Playwright does all the talking.

(At curtain, we see Playwright *sitting at computer and keyboard at SR. At USC stands* Teen 1, Teen 2, *and* Teen 3. *They are standing in a straight line with their backs to audience, in neutral positions.)*

Playwright *(always to self)*: OK, OK. I've got to write this sketch and get it to Pastor [insert local youth pastor or youth leader's name] for this week's teen group. OK, the theme is sin and the consequences of our actions. *(Pondering)* Consequences. Sin. *(Starts typing)* Sin.

*(*Teen 1 *turns around and walks around stage with an ugly face, imitating a monster— plays it big. Typing and talking at once)*

Sin prowls around our lives, trying to destroy us.

*(*Teens 2 *and 3 'unfreeze' and turn DS.* Teen 1 *chases them around stage, all very melodramatic. Think old time silent movies à la villain with curly mustaches, etc.)*

Sin tries to catch us and, er, um, uh, do bad things. To us. And stuff.

*(*Teen 1 *starts choking* Teens 2 *and 3.)*

Wait.

*(*Teens *freeze; no typing now.)*

Man. This *stinks!*

*(*Playwright *hits the keyboard like he/she is deleting what they just typed.)*

Delete, delete, delete.

(As keys are hit, Teens *go backward in their movements that they just made, i.e.,* Teen 1 *un-chokes the other two, they run backwards away from* Teen 1, *etc., and then* Teens *all return to their original spots, with backs to audience. All done like a video running backward. Pause.* Playwright *ponders.)*

OK, that didn't work. Hmmm. Sin. Sin. *(*Teen 1 *turns around again, like the monster, thinking it's his/her 'cue,' starts to run again.)* No, not that again. *(*Teen 1 *stops, returns to original spot.)* Well, maybe. *(*Teen 1 *turns back around and starts with the monster.)* Nah.

*(*Teen 1 *gives* Playwright *a 'look' and turns back again.)*

Wait! Got it! *(Starts typing/talking rapidly.)* OK, OK. We do the devil and angel on the shoulder thing. So, we have a teen *(*Teen 3 *turns and comes DSC)* and uh, a devil and an angel appear on their shoulders.

*(*Teens 1 *and 2 come up behind* Teen 3 *and put their hands on each of* Teen 3's *shoulders. The one playing the devil now has a red sock on their 'shoulder hand', and the one playing the angel now has the white sock on their 'shoulder' hand.* Playwright *continues typing and talking in a high-pitched voice.)*

"Wait young person," says the angel. *(Angel puppet is now 'speaking' onstage.)* "Don't do anything you will regret. You can be good. And kind. And stuff." *(Voice changes to gruff, hoarse, and devil puppet starts.)* "Don't listen to her. She is *so* boring. Have you seen her Facebook profile picture? Back away from the donuts girlfriend, you know what I am sayin'?" *(Angel responds.)* "Oh yeah? At least I'm not Twittering about *everything* I am doing at the moment. 'Oh, I just sneezed.' 'Oh, I just heard a dog barking,' 'Oh, I just had gas.' 'Oh, I . . .'" *(Devil voice.)* "Oh, you wanna go? Bring it, goody two-shoes!" *(Angel now.)* "Really? Really? It's *on!*"

(Puppets start fighting in front of Teen 3's *face, while* Playwright *makes fighting sounds for a few minutes, then stops.)*

Wait. *(Puppets stop fighting and all three* Teens *freeze.)* Uhhh, yeah. *(Sarcastically)* That'll work. *(Sigh.)* Back to the drawing board.

(Same deleting like last scene, and Teens *doing the backward video thing per what they just did and finally return to original positions.)*

Maybe the girlfriend is actually a woman from the future recounting what happened when she was a teen and was talking to her boyfriend about how she sinned in high school and it ruined her life in the future, and then they both get into this cool time machine and . . .

*(*Teens 1 *and* 2 *just stare at* Playwright *with puzzled looks.* Playwright *stops typing, reading the computer screen.)* Whoa. Man, that's worse than the puppets! Ugh. *(Same deleting like last scene,* Teens *going rapidly backwards per what they just did and finally return to original positions, although with less energy this time.)*

Sin. Sin. *(*Teen 1 *turns and makes very half-hearted monster.)* Maybe—show them how sin started! Adam and Eve are in the garden. *(*Teens 2 *and* 3 *turn and walk around as if they are in awe, but also trying to cover their bodies.)* Then Satan, in the form of a snake, tempts Eve with the apple that God told her and Adam never to eat. *(*Teen 1 *acts like a snake and gives* Teen 2 *the apple. She eats it.* Teen 3 *hits his head.)* Duh! Then God kicks them out of the garden. *(*Teens 2 *and* 3 *cross stage, heads hung low,* Teen 1 *struts around.)* And then—and then— *(in great frustration)* that's all I got! Ugh! *(*Teens *throw up their hands, and now refuse to go to neutral positions, start to leave the stage in disgust.)*

This is just not working. How can I communicate how serious sin is and its consequences . . . and how serious God takes it. I—wait, wait. *One* more time. *(*Teens *stop. Look at each other, then reluctantly return to neutral positions.)*

Jesus came to earth *(*Teen 1 *turns and walks DSC, no goofing around now)* to tell us all about His Father's love. *(*Teen 2 *and* 3 *now join* Teen 1. Teen 2 *and* 3 *sit at* Teen 1's *feet and look up as* Teen 1 *pretends to be teaching them. Pause as this unfolds.)* But soon the religious leaders of the day *(*Teen 2 *and* 3 *suddenly take on an ugly demeanor, stand up, grab* Teen 1 *and push him DSR)* hated Jesus because He said love, not laws, was most important.

They got the Romans *(*Teens 2 *and* 3 *pretend to wave in unseen soldiers and point at* Teen 2*)* to agree to have Jesus put to death. *(*Teen 2 *and* 3 *drag* Teen 1 *to DSC. There,* Teen 1 *stands perfectly still, head and arms, hands straight down.* Teen 3 *comes up behind* Teen 1, *while* Teen 2 *takes a few steps away.)* Jesus was nailed to a cross.

18

(Teen 3 *holds their arms straight out from their sides, imitating a cross.* Teen 2 *then moves in. She takes each of* Teen 1's *hands and makes a quick black circle—using a black marker—in the center of each of* Teen 1's *hands, and then slaps* Teen 1's *hands back onto the outstretched arms of* Teen 3. Teen 1 *keeps his hands pressed back against* Teen 3's *arms.* Teen 2 *then steps back again and freezes. Pause for effect.*)

There, God provided forgiveness for every bad attitude and action committed against Him . . . in other words, sin. On the cross, Jesus took on our sin as His own because He loved us enough to make a way for us all to get back to God. When Jesus was about to die, He said, "Father, forgive them. *(Pause.* Teen 2 *puts her hands to her face. Pause.)* It is finished. Father, take me in your arms." And God did.

(Teen 1 *goes limp and falls back into* Teens 3's *arms.* Teen 3 *catches him, and* Teen 2 *comes over to help.* Teen 2 *and 3 then lower* Teen 1 *to floor, and all freeze. Pause.* Teen 2 *and 3 pull pre-placed black fabric up from floor and, over the still prone* Teen 1, *they flap the fabric.*)

A strong storm started and all scattered. Slowly, the storm subsided *(flapping slows gradually and fabric eventually is laid on top of* Teen 1*)* and a tomb became Jesus' home.

(Teens 2 *and 3 kneel next to* Teen 1, *and hang heads and freeze. Blackout. Pause. In dark,* Teen 1 *exits.* Teens 2 *and 3 take white fabric and lay it on top of bunched up black fabric, to make it look like* Teen 1 *may still be there.* Teen 2 *and 3 lay on floor as if sleeping. Lights up.*)

On the third day, His followers came and found . . . life!

(Teens 2 *and 3 waken, look around, then point at white sheet. They slowly pull it up and examine it, giving each other questioning looks.* Teen 2 *holds up the white fabric,* Teen 3 *holds up black fabric, again, questioning looks to each other. During this time* Teen 1 *re-enters unseen, wearing a white sash.* Teen 1 *walks up to* Teen 3. Teen 2 *and 3 now see* Teen 1 *and are amazed and step back.* Teen 1 *goes up to* Teen 2 *and takes the black fabric, balls it up and throws it off DSL.* Teen 1 *then shows them the marks on his hands. They hug, and then all three slowly exit. Pause.*)

Sin—keeps us separated from God. The blood of Jesus, bringing us back. *(Pause, stops typing.)* Resurrecting . . . our relationship with God. *(Long pause)*

Huh. *(Pause)* This . . . this wasn't so hard after all. *(Peers at computer screen, hits one final key, then)* Saved.

(*Slow blackout as* Playwright *freezes.*)

19

Sketch for Teens or Adults

A Process of Finding
by Heidi Petak

Running Time: Approximately 4 minutes

Themes: Salvation, Search for God

Synopsis: A woman struggles to find meaning in life, embracing various worldly "truths," resisting God until the witness of Christians and the love of Jesus breaks through her skepticism.

Cast:
> STEPHANIE—Female, searching for truth
> VOICE 1—Male or female
> VOICE 2—Male or female
> VOICE 3—Male or female

Props:
> Black clothing
> Chair or square cube
> Black cloth
> White clothing

Production Note: The three Voices are positioned behind Stephanie and speak in stage whispers. Stephanie sits wrapped in a black cloth for the majority of the sketch. As she is freed by the truth, she begins to unwrap herself, revealing white clothing and standing unhindered on the final lines.

(When the lights rise, all actors have their heads down.)

VOICE 1 *(raising head)*: My heart kept beating.

VOICE 2 *(raising head)*: Lungs kept breathing.

VOICE 3 *(raising head)*: Walking through life.

VOICE 2: A dead soul on the inside,

VOICE 1: Feeling my way

(Blackout)

ALL VOICES: In the dark.

VOICE 2: Doubt,

VOICE 3: Confusion,

STEPHANIE: It's all a *process* of finding myself.

(Backlights fade up)

VOICE 1: Trapped by my pride,

VOICE 3: My selfishness,

STEPHANIE: I've gotta do what's right for me.

VOICE 2: Behind my padlock of fear,

VOICE 3: Afraid to give,

VOICE 1: Afraid to love.

(Foreground lights fade up)

STEPHANIE: You can't trust anybody these days.

VOICE 3: Navigating an earthly maze

VOICE 2: I played by earthly rules.

ALL VOICES: Earthly rules.

STEPHANIE: Look. I have to find my own truth.

VOICE 1: A baited trap,

VOICE 2: Open mind,

ALL VOICES: Empty heart.

STEPHANIE: I told you . . . it's all a process of *finding* myself.

VOICE 3: God sent

VOICE 1: His only Son.

STEPHANIE *(angrily):* Don't give *me* your Christian . . .

VOICE 3: Can't you see?

STEPHANIE: You see what you want to see.

VOICE 2: I was blind.

VOICE 3: Can't you hear?

STEPHANIE: Hear what?

VOICE 1: He's calling you.

VOICE 3: Calling you.

VOICE 2: Calling you.

STEPHANIE: Stop! I hear what I want to hear!

VOICE 2: He's knocking.

VOICE 3: He's drawing you.

STEPHANIE: No. It's all a process of finding *myself.*

VOICE 1: And what then?

VOICE 2: A dead end

VOICE 1: For a dead soul.

STEPHANIE: Who are you to tell me . . . ?

VOICE 3: I was dead,

VOICE 2: He gave me life.

VOICE 1: I was blind,

VOICE 3: He gave me sight.

STEPHANIE *(with wonder)*: I keep meeting all these Christians.

VOICE 2: He's joy.

VOICE 3: He's peace.

(Foreground lights brighten)

ALL VOICES: He's life.

STEPHANIE *(pause)*: He's life? *(Slowly begins to unwrap)*

VOICE 3: It's Jesus' hand that touched me,

VOICE 2: Drew me to Himself.

VOICE 3: His eyes that loved me,

ALL VOICES: Really loved me,

VOICE 2: Broke through my selfishness,

VOICE 3: My doubt,

VOICE 1: My confusion.

VOICE 3: He touched my soul.

VOICE 2: And gave me

ALL *(including STEPHANIE, standing now in white)*: Life.

STEPHANIE: It's all a process of finding . . . *(stops herself, then begins again)* It's all a process of being found by . . .

ALL: Jesus.

Blackout

Service Ideas

Christ's Betrayal and Passion

A Choral Reading

by Celeste Montgomery

Running Time: 45 minutes to 1 hour

Scriptures: Matthew 26:14-50; Luke 22:14-23:56

Synopsis: Jerusalem, 33 AD; the events of the crucifixion; action takes place over a 24-hour period.

Cast:

NARRATOR—Male or female

JUDAS—Male, 20s

JESUS—Male, 30s

HIGH PRIEST—Male, 55 or older

PILATE—Male, 55 or older

DISCIPLE/CROWD VOICE 1—Male or female, 20s-30s

DISCIPLE/CROWD VOICE 2—Male or female, 20s-30s

DISCIPLE/CROWD VOICE 3—Male or female, 20s-30s

ACCUSER 1/CRIMINAL 1—Male, 30s or older

ACCUSER 2/CRIMINAL 2—Male, 30s or older

WEEPING WOMEN—Any number of female adults, at least 3 for full sound

ELDERS/CROWD/CHORUS—Any number of mixed adults, at least 5 for full sound

Act 1

Setting: Before any congregation: sanctuary, auditorium, or stage

(Readers are assembled in a semi-circle, and may either hold binders or have scripts resting on music stands in front of them. JESUS is at center, CRIMINALS 1 and 2 on his left and right, respectively. The NARRATOR stands on the end, SR or set apart from the others. Other readers should be placed so that voices are equally distributed as they read. Music that enhances the action may be played underneath the reading.)

NARRATOR: Then one of the twelve disciples—the one named Judas Iscariot—went to the chief priests and asked,

JUDAS: What will you give me if I betray Jesus to you?

NARRATOR *(to the sound of coins):* They counted out thirty silver coins and gave them to him. From then on, Judas was looking for a good chance to hand Jesus over to them. On the first day of the Festival of Unleavened Bread, the disciples came to Jesus and asked Him,

DISCIPLE 1: Where do You want us to get the Passover meal ready for You?

NARRATOR: The disciples did as Jesus had told them and prepared the Passover meal. When it was evening, Jesus and the twelve disciples sat down to eat. During this meal, Jesus said,

JESUS: I tell you, one of you will betray Me.

NARRATOR: The disciples were very upset and began to ask Him, one after another,

DISCIPLES 1/2/3: Surely, Lord, You don't mean me? Is it I, Lord? Lord, it cannot be me!

NARRATOR: Jesus answered,

JESUS *(with* JUDAS, *simultaneously dipping motion):* One who dips his bread in the dish with Me will betray Me.

NARRATOR: Judas, the traitor, spoke up.

JUDAS: Surely, Teacher, You don't mean me?

NARRATOR: Jesus answered,

JESUS: So you say.

NARRATOR: While they were eating, Jesus took a piece of bread, gave a prayer of thanks, broke it, and gave it to His disciples.

JESUS: Take and eat it,

NARRATOR: He said;

JESUS: This is My body.

NARRATOR: Then He took a cup, gave thanks to God, and gave it to them.

JESUS: Drink it, all of you.

NARRATOR: He said,

JESUS: This is My blood, which seals God's covenant, My blood poured out for many for the forgiveness of sins. I tell you, I will never again drink this wine until the day I drink the new wine with you in My Father's Kingdom.

NARRATOR: Then they sang a hymn and went out to the Mount of Olives.

(Congregation may sing a selected hymn. The author suggests "Abide with Me.")

Act 2

(Readers take their places as in Act 1.)

NARRATOR: Jesus was still speaking when Judas, one of the twelve disciples, arrived. With him was a large crowd armed with swords and clubs, and sent by the chief priests and the elders. The traitor had given the crowd a signal:

JUDAS: The Man I kiss is the One you want. Arrest Him!

NARRATOR: Judas went straight to Jesus and said,

JUDAS: Peace be with You, Teacher,

NARRATOR: and kissed Him. Jesus answered,

JESUS: Be quick about it, friend!

NARRATOR: Then they came up, arrested Jesus, and held Him tight. Then Jesus spoke to the crowd,

JESUS: Did you have to come to Me with swords and clubs to capture Me as though I were an outlaw? Everyday I sat down and taught in the Temple, and you did not arrest Me. But all this has happened in order to make come true what the prophets wrote in the Scriptures.

NARRATOR: Then all the disciples left Him and ran away. Those who had arrested Jesus took Him to the house of Caiaphas, the High Priest, where the teachers of the law and the elders gathered together. The chief priests and the whole council tried to find some false evidence against Jesus to put Him to death. Finally, two men stepped up and said,

ACCUSER 1: This Man said, "I am able to tear down God's Temple . . .

ACCUSER 2: and three days later build it back up."

NARRATOR: The High Priest stood up and said to Jesus,

HIGH PRIEST: Have You no answers to give to the accusation against You?

NARRATOR: But Jesus kept quiet. Again the High Priest spoke to Him.

HIGH PRIEST: In the name of the living God, I now put You under oath: tell us if You are the Messiah, the Son of God?

NARRATOR: Jesus answered him,

JESUS: So you say. But I tell all of you from this time on you will see the Son of Man sitting at the right side of the Almighty and coming on the clouds of heaven.

NARRATOR: At this the High Priest tore his clothes and said,

HIGH PRIEST *(with great indignation and righteous anger)*: Blasphemy! We don't need any more witnesses! You have just heard blasphemy! What do you think?

NARRATOR: And the elders answered,

ELDERS *(with self-righteous conviction)*: He is guilty and must die!

NARRATOR: Early in the morning all the chief priests and the elders made their plans against Jesus to put Him to death. They put Him in chains, led Him off, and handed Him over to Pilate, the Roman Governor.

(Out of silence, a rhythmic rumbling of CROWD/CHORUS *begins. To give the illusion of a crowd approaching, rumbling is low at first, and gradually crescendos into rabble which continues through the first* PILATE *encounter.)*

NARRATOR: Then the assembly rose as a body and brought Jesus before Pilate. They began to accuse Him saying,

CROWD VOICE 1: We found this Man perverting our nation, forbidding us to pay taxes to the emperor, and saying that He himself is the Messiah, a king.

(Rhythmic rumbling volume of CROWD/CHORUS *peaks then diminishes again, still audible under the dialogue.)*

NARRATOR: Then Pilate asked Him,

PILATE: Are You the King of the Jews?

NARRATOR: He answered,

JESUS: You say so.

(Rhythmic rumbling volume of CROWD/CHORUS *peaks then diminishes again, still audible under the dialogue.)*

NARRATOR: Then Pilate said to the chief priests and the crowds,

PILATE: I find no basis for an accusation against this Man.

NARRATOR: But they were insistent and said,

(Rhythmic rumbling volume of CROWD/CHORUS *peaks then diminishes again, still audible under the dialogue.)*

CROWD VOICE 2: He stirs up the people by teaching throughout all Judea, from Galilee where He began even to this place.

NARRATOR: When Pilate heard this, he asked whether the Man was a Galilean. And when he learned that Jesus was under Herod's jurisdiction, Pilate sent Him off to Herod, who was himself in Jerusalem at that time.

*(*CROWD/CHORUS *rumble dies away.)*

When Herod saw Jesus, he was very glad, for he had wanted to see Jesus for a long time. Herod had heard about Him and was hoping to see Him perform some sign. He questioned Him at some length, but Jesus gave him no answer. The chief priests and the scribes stood by, vehemently accusing Jesus.

(The following sentences are spit with venom from members of the CROWD/CHORUS, *overlapping one with another, using the hard consonant sounds like darts. Again, rise and fall of rabble to continue under the dialogue that follows.)*

CROWD/CHORUS: "You are accused!"

"King of the Jews?"

"You pervert the law!"

"You disrespect us with Your silence!"

"You must be punished for Your crime."

"Shameful charlatan!"

NARRATOR: Even Herod with his soldiers treated Him with contempt and mocked Him; then Herod put an elegant robe on Jesus, and sent Him back to Pilate.

(CROWD/CHORUS *rumble, now peppered with cruel laughter, dies away.*)

That same day Herod and Pilate became friends with each other; before this they had been enemies.

(*Congregation or choir may sing a selected hymn. The author suggests "Ah, Holy Jesus," by Johann Herrmann.*)

Pilate then called together the chief priests, the leaders, and the people, and said to them,

PILATE: You brought me this Man as one who was perverting the people; and here I have examined Him in your presence and have not found this Man guilty of any of your charges against Him. Neither has Herod, for he sent Him back to us. Indeed, He has done nothing to deserve death. I will therefore have Him flogged and release Him.

NARRATOR: Then they all shouted out together,

CROWD VOICE 3: Away with this fellow!

CROWD/CHORUS (*in unison*): Release Barabbas for us!

NARRATOR: This was a man who had been put in prison for an insurrection that had taken place in the city, and for murder. Pilate, wanting to release Jesus, addressed them again; but they kept shouting.

(*Following cries are overlapping, expressed first with rhythmic unity, and evolving into a jagged and reckless din.*)

CROWD/CHORUS: "Crucify, crucify Him!"

"Crucify, crucify Him!"

"Crucify, crucify Him!"

"Crucify, crucify Him!"

"Crucify, crucify Him!"

"Crucify, crucify Him!"

"Crucify, crucify Him!"

(Shouting continues at a volume which requires the NARRATOR *and* PILATE *to raise their voices to be heard.)*

NARRATOR: A third time he said to them,

PILATE: Why, what evil has He done? I have found in Him no grounds for the sentence of death; I will therefore have Him flogged and then release Him.

NARRATOR: But they kept urgently demanding with loud shouts that He should be crucified; and their voices prevailed.

(Shouts of the CROWD/CHORUS *fade away.)*

So Pilate gave his verdict that their demand should be granted. He released the man they asked for, the one who had been put in prison for insurrection and murder, and he handed Jesus over as they wished. As they led Him away, they seized a man, Simon of Cyrene, who was coming from the country, and they laid the cross on him, and made him carry it behind Jesus.

(Congregation or choir may sing a selected hymn. The author suggests "What Wondrous Love Is This?")

A great number of people followed Jesus, and among them were women who were beating their breasts and wailing for Him.

(Sounds of heart-rending grief and weeping rise. The following phrases may be heard, overlapping and mixed with moans, wails, and crying.)

WEEPING WOMEN: "No! He has done no wrong!"

"This is a good man!"

"He healed my daughter!"

"He is innocent."

"What sorrow falls upon His mother and on us!"

*(*WEEPING WOMEN *continue wailing and moaning under the dialogue that follows.)*

NARRATOR: But Jesus turned to them and said,

JESUS: Daughters of Jerusalem, do not weep for Me, for weep for yourselves and for your children. For the days are surely coming when they will say, "Blessed are the barren, and the wombs that never bore, and the breasts that never nursed." Then they will begin to say to the mountains, "Fall on us"; and to the hills, "Cover us." For if they do this when the wood is green, what will happen when it is dry?

(Greater sounds of weeping and despair rise after hearing these words. The wailing diminishes into soft moaning throughout the crucifixion.)

NARRATOR: Two others also, who were criminals, were led away to be put to death with Him. When they came to the place that is called The Skull, they crucified Jesus there with the criminals, one on His right and one on His left. Then Jesus said,

JESUS: Father, forgive them; for they do not know what they are doing.

NARRATOR: And they cast lots to divide His clothing. And the people stood by, watching; but the leaders scoffed at Him, saying,

CROWD VOICE 2: He saved others; let Him save himself if He is the Messiah of God, His chosen One!

NARRATOR: The soldiers also mocked Him, coming up and offering Him sour wine, and saying,

CROWD VOICE 3: If You are the King of the Jews, save Yourself!

NARRATOR: There was also an inscription over Him. "This is the King of the Jews." One of the criminals who was hanging there kept deriding Him and saying,

CRIMINAL 1: Are You not the Messiah? Save Yourself and us!

NARRATOR: But the other rebuked him, saying,

CRIMINAL 2: Do you not fear God, since you are under the same sentence of condemnation? And we indeed have been condemned justly, for we are getting what we deserve for our deeds, but this Man has done nothing wrong.

NARRATOR: Then he said,

CRIMINAL 2: Jesus, remember me when You come into Your kingdom.

NARRATOR: Jesus replied,

JESUS: Truly I tell you, today you will be with Me in Paradise.

NARRATOR: It was now about noon, and darkness came over the whole land until three in the afternoon, while the sun's light failed; and the curtain of the Temple was torn in two. Then Jesus, crying with a loud voice, said,

JESUS: Father, in Your hands I commend My spirit.

NARRATOR: Having said this, He breathed His last. When the centurion saw what had taken place, he praised God and said,

CROWD VOICE 3: Certainly, this Man was innocent.

NARRATOR: And when all the crowds who had gathered there for this spectacle saw what had taken place, they returned home, beating their breasts. But all His acquaintances, including the women who had followed Him from Galilee, stood at a distance, watching these things.

(A lonely remaining moan emerges from one of the WEEPING WOMEN. *It disintegrates into silence.)*

Mary's Easter Experience

A Monologue

by Celeste Montgomery

Running Time: Approximately 5 to 6 minutes

Scripture: John 20:1-18

Synopsis: A monologue for Easter morning

Cast:

> MARY MAGDALENE—Disciple of Jesus, the first to report the news of His resurrection

Part 1

Discovery

Setting: The path to the garden and the tomb where the body of Jesus was laid; dark dawn of Sunday morning after Jesus' death.

(MARY MAGDALENE enters from SL door of the sanctuary. Her head is covered with a black shawl. She carries a spice bowl and lighted lantern. During the following speech, she walks slowly through the aisles of the congregation, eventually moving up the center aisle to arrive at the "tomb," CS.)

MARY: The sun's not yet up. Will the sun ever rise? I haven't slept for three days. I haven't slept since . . . since my Lord died. And this last one has been the longest night for me. So I occupied myself with grinding spices for His body, and now I take them to His tomb. I cannot wait for the sun.

It is so difficult to bear this loss. I feel so helpless! And, so angry!

He was to be our King. Our Messiah. He was to lead us. It never entered my mind that He should die. That He could die. Never was there a Man as good as He who has lived on this earth. And that He should die and leave us. Leave me!

How could God allow this to happen? And why? What are we to do now?

(MARY arrives at the tomb.)

Ah! Someone has not been sleeping either and come here before me. The stone has been already rolled away.

(She looks in.)

He is not here! His body has been stolen! Who would do such a thing!

(Calling out.)

Peter! John! Come quickly! They have stolen His body! It is not here!

(She watches them look inside and reacts.)

What? You see what has been done and you simply go home? Where is your courage? Do you intend on hiding in that upper room forever? Why should you be so afraid to find out what happened? Our Lord is dead, so what is there to live for anyway?

(She breaks down into sobs. Sensing someone near, she addresses Him.)

Oh, Sir! They have taken my Lord and I don't know where they have laid His body.

You must be the gardener. Please! Have You taken Him? If You have, please tell me where He is. I have spices for Him . . .

(She stops and looks up, reacts as she recognizes the voice that says her name.)

Rabbi! Oh Teacher! Is it You? Does my lack of sleep cause me to imagine You?

(Reaching out for Him.)

No, it is You! My Lord, You are not dead! You are alive, risen!

(She falls on her knees, laughing through tears.)

Yes, yes, I will obey and release You. But only because You bid me. And I will go to Your disciples and tell them what You have said.

(MARY exits SR side of the sanctuary.)

Part 2

Proclamation

Setting: Upper room where the disciples are hiding.

(MARY enters with nervous excitement, now wearing a white shawl. She addresses the disciples—who are the congregation.)

MARY: Shalom, everyone! I . . . I have been to the tomb already this morning. I was bringing spices. I was surprised to find the stone already rolled away. Ah, Peter told you already.

I have something else to tell you.

(Begins giving this speech to one person, in a bit of a whisper, and gathering strength, confidence, and volume as she tells the story, gradually addressing everyone.)

I have seen the Lord! I thought He was the gardener, but, He said, "Mary," and I knew it was Him. There He was, standing right in front of me, glowing bright and alive as the snow on Mount Sinai. I have seen the Lord!

I can hardly believe it myself! I have seen the Lord! He is no longer dead, but He is risen!

I heard Him with my own ears, and clung to Him with my own arms. I have seen the Lord!

31

He asked me to come and tell you this:

"I ascend to My Father and your Father, and My God and your God."

I have seen the Lord!

Christ has risen . . . He is risen indeed!

(Developing a rhythm, with the help of percussion, MARY *encourages the disciples to join her in the proclamation. Perhaps she may begin to lead joyful song of triumph. If dancing in the aisles ensues, it should not be discouraged.)*